S0-BYF-897

THE POWER OF THE
DOUBLE

RYAN LeSTRANGE

CHARISMA
HOUSE

Most CHARISMA HOUSE BOOK GROUP products are available at special quantity discounts for bulk purchase for sales promotions, premiums, fundraising, and educational needs. For details, write Charisma House Book Group, 600 Rinehart Road, Lake Mary, Florida 32746, or telephone (407) 333-0600.

THE POWER OF THE DOUBLE by Ryan LeStrange
Published by Charisma House
Charisma Media/Charisma House Book Group
600 Rinehart Road
Lake Mary, Florida 32746
www.charismahouse.com

This book or parts thereof may not be reproduced in any form, stored in a retrieval system, or transmitted in any form by any means—electronic, mechanical, photocopy, recording, or otherwise—without prior written permission of the publisher, except as provided by United States of America copyright law.

Unless otherwise noted, all Scripture quotations are taken from the New American Standard Bible, copyright © 1960, 1962, 1963, 1968, 1971, 1972, 1973, 1975, 1977, 1995 by The Lockman Foundation. Used by permission. www.Lockman.org

Scripture quotations marked ESV are from the Holy Bible, English Standard Version. Copyright © 2001 by

Crossway Bibles, a division of Good News Publishers. Used by permission.

Scripture quotations marked KJV are from the King James Version of the Bible.

Scripture quotations marked NKJV are taken from the New King James Version®. Copyright © 1982 by Thomas Nelson. Used by permission. All rights reserved.

Copyright © 2019 by Ryan LeStrange
All rights reserved

Visit the author's website at www.ryanlestrange.com.

Library of Congress Cataloging-in-Publication Data: An application to register this book for cataloging has been submitted to the Library of Congress. International Standard Book Number: 978-1-62999-663-9 E-book ISBN: 978-1-62999-664-6

While the author has made every effort to provide accurate internet addresses at the time of publication, neither the publisher nor the author assumes any responsibility for errors or for changes that occur after publication. Further, the publisher does not have any control over and does not assume any responsibility for author or third-party websites or their content.

19 20 21 22 23 — 987654321
Printed in the United States of America

CONTENTS

Chapter 1

GOD WILL MORE THAN RESTORE

W HILE I MINISTERED in another nation, some of my spiritual sons and daughters began singing a song written by an artist from Africa. The song's prophetic message hit my spirit deeply as the congregation sang of the "double-double" increase God wants to bring forth.

Over the next several months, I thought about the "double-double" song and played it many times. Then, when I was preaching in South Africa, the church sang the song during worship. At the time, I was meditating on a prophetic assignment and upcoming milestone in my life. As I pondered this with the song reverberating in my ear, the Lord clearly instructed me to write a prophetic book about the double-double.

The idea of *double* is found throughout the Scriptures. The following verse is an excellent example:

> Return to the stronghold, O prisoners who
> have the hope; this very day I am declaring
> that I will restore double to you.
>
> —ZECHARIAH 9:12

In this verse God is telling His people to believe for double restoration. We often fight fierce battles, believing for the return of that which the enemy has stolen. I want to prophesy and declare over you that God is not just returning what was taken—I want you to set your faith on receiving a minimum of double!

What if you got back double after every attack? Can you imagine your finances, joy, health, prophetic insight, and wisdom doubling? This is not just a catchy word; it is the *Word of the Lord*, and it speaks of restoration. *Merriam-Webster* defines the word *restore* as "give back, return; to put or bring back into existence or use; to bring back to or put back into a former or original state: renew; to put again in possession of something."[1]

Get that sealed in your spirit! The enemy has snatched things from your life, but God wants to bring restoration. He desires to give it back to you in double-double capacity! He wants to bless you so hugely that you experience massive overflow. There are words heaven has spoken over you, and some of them have caused mega-warfare to erupt in your life. The hordes of hell have tried to pry those words from your hands.

Demonic forces have attacked your prophetic promise in an attempt to get you to abandon your course.

But true prophetic words empower purpose and equip you for battle, which is why the apostle Paul charged Timothy to wage a good warfare with the word of the Lord!

> This command I entrust to you, Timothy, my son, in accordance with the prophecies previously made concerning you, that by them you fight the good fight.
>
> —1 TIMOTHY 1:18

When heaven speaks, faith is established and the pathway is made clear. You see where you are headed, and you have the ability to believe God for it. Warfare erupts to get you into doubt and unbelief about the things heaven has clearly spoken over your life. This is a tactical strategy of the enemy.

Satan wants to keep you from recognizing your prophetic destiny. He wants to get you wandering through life without clear definition or a concise direction. He wants to dim your vision and mute your hearing. This is an evil strategy to disrupt the progression of God's plans for you.

It is time to re-dig the prophetic wells in your life. It is time to boldly and unashamedly stand upon the Word of the Lord. If heaven said it, then it is so! It doesn't matter what Satan or his minions think. There is a double-double restoration available to ignite your prophetic purpose and destiny. There is a double-double blessing of insight and clarity prepared for you and a double-double anointing for accuracy in the realm of the spirit. I believe that even as you read these words, God is once again stirring your sense of balance and direction.

PROPHETIC WORD

I see many people walking straight ahead with their eyes on the prize, but then demonic resistance knocks them off course. They lose their sense of balance and begin to stumble in the realm of the spirit.

I hear the Lord saying, "Hell has attempted to knock you down. Hell has thrown the winds of opposition and adversity at you, but strength and stamina are coming forth. I am clarifying your vision and refocusing your gaze. The warfare has come to get you off track. It has come to alter your vision. I am restoring to you My vision and direction. I am restoring clarity and purpose. I am also reestablishing the sense of urgency in your life concerning My plans and direction. You shall not wander aimlessly. You shall not simply go to and fro, but you shall be on assignment, on task, moving in unison with My proclamation over your life. I am reestablishing My prophetic purpose in you and through you. The battle has been about My purpose for you. The battle has been about My establishing you in prophetic destiny. I am causing your steps to be sure, your gaze fixed, and your mind clear. Receive My restoration. Receive My clarity. Receive My breakthrough. The grip of hell is broken in My glory. The onslaught of the wicked one is halted in My power. This day I am breaking you free and breaking you loose. You shall run and advance boldly in Me. You shall surge forward and rapidly move ahead. Restoration belongs to you. I am the God of restoration. I can and will put it back! I can and will give it back! I can and will bring it back! I am restoring you in My presence and My glory. Worship Me, and seek My face. My presence causes restoration to come forth."

Chapter 2

GLORY LIFTS

W HEN ATTACKS AND losses come—even when our own choices cause us trouble—only God can heal and restore us. We can run to Him and trust Him.

> Come, let us return to the LORD. For He has torn us, but He will heal us; He has wounded us, but He will bandage us. He will revive us after two days; He will raise us up on the third day, that we may live before Him. So let us know, let us press on to know the LORD. His going forth is as certain as the dawn; and He will come to us like the rain, like the spring rain watering the earth.
>
> —HOSEA 6:1–3

As we return to the presence of the Lord, His healing power begins to flow. He heals our areas of discouragement and brings forth restoration in the glory realm. As we worship Him, we should expect the double-double. In the midst of His presence, our wounds are restored, disappointment is broken off, and the glory begins to lift us above our sorrows.

There is a lifting in the glory! Heaven never intended for you to live in the low places. You were not born to be a duck. You were born to be an eagle. Eagles don't stay on the ground. They soar up high. There is a double-double soaring that God wants to bring forth. He wants you to ride the winds of His glory. He will cause your vision and your thoughts to soar higher. He will cause your prayers to come up higher too.

> Yet those who wait for the LORD will gain new strength; they will mount up with wings like eagles, they will run and not get tired, they will walk and not become weary.
>
> —ISAIAH 40:31

Your perspective is vital. If you cannot see from the right perspective, you will become exhausted and discouraged. One mark of spiritual warfare is the limiting of what and how you see. The enemy tries to keep you fastened to the low points. But you were made to arise and win in Jesus!

...and raised us up with Him, and seated us with Him in the heavenly places in Christ Jesus, so that in the ages to come He might show the surpassing riches of His grace in kindness toward us in Christ Jesus.

—EPHESIANS 2:6–7

Expect and confess the lifting! Expect and confess a rise in the glory of God. Praise Him when the chips are down, and He will give you a testimony.

Bless our God, O peoples, and sound His praise abroad, who keeps us in life and does not allow our feet to slip. For You have tried us, O God; You have refined us as silver is refined. You brought us into the net; You laid an oppressive burden upon our loins. *You made men ride over our heads; we went through fire and through water, yet You brought us out into a place of abundance.* I shall come into Your house with burnt offerings; I shall pay You my vows, which my lips uttered and my mouth spoke when I was in distress. I shall offer to You burnt offerings of fat beasts, with the smoke of rams; I shall make an offering of bulls with male goats. Selah.

> Come and hear, all who fear God, and I
> will tell of what He has done for my soul.
> —PSALM 66:8–16, EMPHASIS ADDED

This psalm paints a vivid picture of God's restoration. In the midst of persecution and attacks, the author chooses to lift up his voice! Worship and praise then release the restoration. The double-double is activated by sound. As we praise God and declare His Word, we access the realm of the impossible and the supernatural. Our faith must be spoken. It simply cannot remain silent.

I love the verbiage of verse 12. We are *brought out*! This bringing out is part of the double-double. We are supernaturally delivered from the snare of the wicked one and suddenly brought out of his grip. This is the restoring power of God in action. In and of itself, that would be good. But it gets better. You are brought out and then brought in—to the blessing realm! You are brought into prophetic purpose. You are brought into healing. You are brought into abundance. All of it is part of God's restoring power.

Abundance is not only about receiving. Psalm 66 talks about the offering, which is a key part of the manifestation of the double-double in your life. We must have a vision for the future that empowers our giving. In times of crisis, sowing is vital.

> There is one who scatters, and yet increases all the more, and there is one who withholds what is justly due, and yet it results only in want. The generous man will be prosperous, and he who waters will himself be watered. He who withholds grain, the people will curse him, but blessing will be on the head of him who sells it.
>
> —PROVERBS 11:24–26

You need to sow as if you are *believing* for the double-double. Financial giving is essential! In times of crisis the enemy releases fear and bondage as part of the mental and emotional warfare he wages. You must act in faith and not in fear. You must sow in the midst of the attack! Seed releases power and increase. Increase is released by your seed.

Everything in the kingdom of God begins with seed, and everything is seed activated. This is why we are instructed not to despise the day of small beginnings. Basically the Lord is showing us the day of the seed. Our praise is a seed. Our worship is a seed. Our giving is a seed. Our words and our prayers are seeds. Seeds begin as small things but hold the potential to shake nations.

God never starts us out where we are going to end up. He begins with a small word, thought, or prompting. This is how the kingdom of God is initiated in our lives: in seed form. It is our responsibility to properly steward and water the seed. We have to water the seed with our confession and our worship. We also water the seed with our decrees.

SIX BIBLE VERSES ABOUT GOD'S POWERFUL RESTORATION

Following are six powerful verses about God's restoration. Decree them. Pray and meditate upon them. Let them speak a better and different word over the areas of your life that have been wounded.

1. Psalm 23:3 (ESV): "He restores my soul. He leads me in paths of righteousness for his name's sake."

2. Exodus 21:34 (ESV): "The owner of the pit shall make restoration. He shall give money to its owner, and the dead beast shall be his."

3. Amos 9:14 (ESV): "I will restore the fortunes of my people Israel, and they shall rebuild the ruined cities and inhabit them; they shall plant vineyards and drink their wine, and they shall make gardens and eat their fruit."

4. 2 Corinthians 13:9 (ESV): "For we are glad when we are weak and you are strong. Your restoration is what we pray for."

5. 2 Corinthians 13:11 (ESV): "Finally, brothers, rejoice. Aim for restoration, comfort one another, agree with one another, live in peace; and the God of love and peace will be with you."

6. Galatians 6:1 (ESV): "Brothers, if anyone is caught in any transgression, you who are spiritual should restore him in a spirit of gentleness. Keep watch on yourself, lest you too be tempted."

Chapter 3

THE DOUBLE PORTION

As we explore the prophetic potential of the double-double, there is a particularly interesting mention of *double* in the Bible—it is the double portion. We often think of this from the perspective of fiery Pentecostal meetings in which heightened levels of God's power and presence are being poured out. But there is more.

I love the anointing and the manifest power of God, and I am ready for the increased outpouring of His glory and majesty. I believe this is part of our double-double. There is nothing like the exhilarating and tangible realm of His anointing being poured out. Yet I believe there is something deeper in the concept of the double portion, which is first mentioned in the Jewish law.

> He shall acknowledge the firstborn, the son of
> the unloved, by giving him a double portion

> of all that he has, for he is the beginning of
> his strength; to him belongs the right of the
> firstborn.
>
> —DEUTERONOMY 21:17

In the Law of Moses, the eldest son was entitled to a double portion of the inheritance. If there were three sons, the inheritance would be divided into four parts, and the eldest would receive two of them. Talk about a double-double! I cannot help but think of the prophetic picture here concerning our inheritance through Jesus Christ.

> He rescued us from the domain of darkness,
> and transferred us to the kingdom of His
> beloved Son, in whom we have redemption,
> the forgiveness of sins. He is the image of the
> invisible God, the firstborn of all creation.
>
> —COLOSSIANS 1:13–15

Jesus was the firstborn of all creation, the second Adam, who came to strip the devil of all authority and power. Who gave that power to the enemy? Adam did. Jesus came as fully God and fully man to take back that which Adam handed over to Satan. When He purchased our redemption, Jesus stripped our enemy of the power to hold us captive. He canceled our debt and set us free.

> When you were dead in your transgressions and the uncircumcision of your flesh, He made you alive together with Him, having forgiven us all our transgressions, having canceled out the certificate of debt consisting of decrees against us, which was hostile to us; and He has taken it out of the way, having nailed it to the cross. When He had disarmed the rulers and authorities, He made a public display of them, having triumphed over them through Him.
>
> —Colossians 2:13–15

Jesus disarmed the forces of hell, totally stripping them of their legal rights to humankind. When we are born again, we are born into the full victory of the eldest, who is Jesus! We are born into a place and position of authority. We are born into the victory He won. The enemy must then try to gain access into our lives by getting us to open the door and invite him in.

We don't have to let him in. We have an incorruptible inheritance! Through the covenant of Jesus Christ, we have been given a double portion—an inheritance that empowers us to go forth in His name.

> All authority has been given to Me in heaven and on earth. Go therefore and make disciples of all the nations, baptizing them in the name of the Father and the Son and the

> Holy Spirit, teaching them to observe all that
> I commanded you; and lo, I am with you
> always, even to the end of the age.
>
> —MATTHEW 28:18–20

Jesus said *all* authority was granted to Him. It was not a portion of the authority needed to strip the enemy. It was the full backing of heaven and the majesty of the Father. He executed that total authority by stripping hell of its hold on humanity. Because of that complete work, He then handed the authority to the church, equipping us to rule nations, change humanity, and establish the kingdom of God—not someday, but now. It's not a future promise, but a present reality. The kingdom is already here, and it is alive, active, and full of power.

The double portion is more than an anointing. It is a position in Christ and a place of victory, majesty, and authority. It is an identity and the full assurance of the total and complete redemption of Jesus Christ in our lives.

Ezekiel wrote about the double portion that God granted Joseph in the Promised Land.

> Thus says the Lord GOD, "This shall be the
> boundary by which you shall divide the land
> for an inheritance among the twelve tribes
> of Israel; Joseph shall have two portions. You

shall divide it for an inheritance, each one equally with the other; for I swore to give it to your forefathers, and this land shall fall to you as an inheritance.

—EZEKIEL 47:13–14

God also promised the wandering Israelites a double portion of manna on the sixth day of each week. He swore to give them increased provision so they could enter into His rest on the seventh day.

Then the LORD said to Moses, "Behold, I will rain bread from heaven for you; and the people shall go out and gather a day's portion every day, that I may test them, whether or not they will walk in My instruction. On the sixth day, when they prepare what they bring in, it will be twice as much as they gather daily."

—EXODUS 16:4–5

These passages from Ezekiel and Exodus are prophetic pictures of a double-double provision that is available to you and me through the covenant we have with our God. We can rest fully in Him and in the total work of Jesus Christ!

DOUBLE FOR TROUBLE

No one gets through this life without experiencing trouble. For God's people, however, trouble is not the final word. Not only does He promise to be with us in trouble; He also reminds us that we will be joyful again.

> Instead of your shame you will have a double portion, and instead of humiliation they will shout for joy over their portion. Therefore they will possess a double portion in their land, everlasting joy will be theirs. For I, the LORD, love justice, I hate robbery in the burnt offering; and I will faithfully give them their recompense and make an everlasting covenant with them. Then their offspring will be known among the nations, and their descendants in the midst of the peoples. All who see them will recognize them because they are the offspring whom the LORD has blessed.
>
> —ISAIAH 61:7–9

I love these verses written to God's people! He promised to bring us out of shame and bondage and give us a double portion. If you have been stripped, attacked, lied about, or lied to, you need to grab this promise. Shame will not remain in the majestic and wonderful presence of Jesus.

The dictionary defines *shame* as "a painful emotion caused by consciousness of guilt, shortcoming, or impropriety; a condition of humiliating disgrace or disrepute; something that brings censure or reproach; *also*: something to be regretted."[1] The devil tries to put shame on us for past sins and failures. He uses shame and guilt to release false identity in an attempt to keep us in bondage. Shame is a force from hell that is designed to weigh us down and keep us from entering the promises of God.

The Lord responds by saying that instead of shame, guilt, painful emotions, or humiliation, you shall have a double portion. You *shall* receive your inheritance. This is an all-encompassing promise—a fullness-of-identity promise with all the benefits that Jesus restored on our behalf. Therefore, speak forth the double-double! Speak forth your inheritance. Decree an end to shame, and partner often with this promise of heaven over your life:

> Return to the stronghold, O prisoners who have the hope; this very day I am declaring that I will restore double to you.
>
> —ZECHARIAH 9:12

The Lord tells us to return to the stronghold! Return to the fortified place of His presence. Return to the rock of His Word. Return to the place of worship. The

21

enemy does all he can to divert our attention by sowing seeds of heaviness. Go back to the rock, who is Jesus! Go back to the place of His promise. Stand in the midst of His glory, and worship Him for your deliverance.

It would be good news just to get back what you lost, but the Lord did not stop there! He says He will restore double to you! *Double!*

I decree the double in every area of your financial life: double increase, double restoration, and double miracles! I decree double over your health. I decree double peace. I decree double blessing on every area of your life! May the power of God's mighty hand sweep over you and bring forth the double. He did it in Job's life!

> The LORD restored the fortunes of Job when he prayed for his friends, and the LORD increased all that Job had twofold.
>
> —JOB 42:10

As Job prayed for his friends, God brought forth the double. Satan had attacked every area of Job's life, unleashing one of the most excruciating trials recorded in the Word of God. Yet Job refused to give up on God and His glory. When the Lord's power showed up, He not only restored what Job had lost; *He brought back double*! This is the promise of God over your life. Satan has to pay back more than what he took.

Some of the Bible's greatest testimonies followed profound heartbreak. This was true of Hannah, who loved the Lord but had a terrible burden: she was barren.

> But to Hannah he would give a double portion, for he loved Hannah, but the LORD had closed her womb. Her rival, however, would provoke her bitterly to irritate her, because the LORD had closed her womb.
>
> —1 SAMUEL 1:5–6

Hannah's womb was not called to barrenness; she was called to birth a great prophet. Yet for years her womb was shut. We often experience these types of struggles. We know there is great prophetic destiny within us, but we cannot seem to get it to come forth. The barrenness brings heartrending pain and feelings of inadequacy.

Hannah faced great shame. In ancient Israel people believed that a large family signified God's blessing. Hannah's lack of children was a source of intense humiliation. Not only was she childless, but her husband's other wife taunted and harassed her.

Isn't this always the case when you are battling in an area of your life? The devil sends someone to speak his vile accusations against you and keep you bound outside of your identity in God. The double-double is about coming into the fullness of who you are and all that you are called to do and be. But you will never enter this realm fully without facing some accusers, mockers, and attackers.

Hannah did not take her case to man. She took her case to God, praying so fervently that Eli the priest thought she was drunk. She knew that heaven held her answer! When Eli asked her what was wrong, she explained that she was pouring out her heart to the Lord.

> Then Eli answered and said, "Go in peace; and may the God of Israel grant your petition that you have asked of Him." She said, "Let your maidservant find favor in your sight." So the woman went her way and ate, and her face was no longer sad.
>
> —1 SAMUEL 1:17–18

Not only would Hannah receive her answer; she would receive double! Not only would barrenness be broken in her life, but she would give birth to Samuel, one of the greatest prophets in all of history. What a potent lesson this is for us! When it looks as if we are struggling and even failing, a nation-shaking assignment may be ready to come forth.

God's double shocks our enemies. God's double causes great things to come forth for despised and ridiculed people. God's double brings glory in the midst of the dry places and the wilderness. God's double will shut the attacker's mouth and bring forth justice.

Hannah contended for the breaking of her barrenness. Do you have unfulfilled promises in your life? Then don't throw in the towel! Do not think that heaven has passed over you. Keep praying. Keep believing. Keep contending. The God of the double is on your side. The God of more than enough is well able to bring you out and touch your barren areas.

Chapter 4

DOUBLE HONOR

W HATEVER WE DEEM valuable we honor by supporting and speaking highly of it. This is true
both within the church and beyond it.

> The elders who rule well are to be considered
> worthy of double honor, especially those who
> work hard at preaching and teaching. For the
> Scripture says, "You shall not muzzle the ox
> while he is threshing," and "The laborer is
> worthy of his wages." Do not receive an accu-
> sation against an elder except on the basis of
> two or three witnesses.
>
> —1 TIMOTHY 5:17–19

In this passage Paul writes about areas of honor
within the church and says elders (seasoned, mature
ones) who preach and teach are worthy of double

honor. Paul is speaking to us about discerning and valuing the gift of God.

DEMONSTRATING HONOR

One of the challenges we face in the church is the way we represent ourselves and our leaders. We often discredit and tear down one another so strongly that the world places no value on us. As believers we are instructed not only to honor those who speak spiritual truths into our lives but to place double honor on them! This means deeming them valuable by speaking highly of them, sowing into their lives, and supporting them.

One aspect of the double honor described in 1 Timothy 5 is to sow and bless financially. Many people struggle with this concept, but if you think about it, it is simple. When you really value something, you are not concerned about the price. You pay more for an item or brand that you like. You pay more for a five-star hotel than a two-star one. That is an earthly measuring system, but God's heavenly measuring system requires no less! He wants us to support the people and ministries we esteem valuable.

The Expositor's Bible Commentary states the following about 1 Timothy 5:17:

Elders, those who directed the affairs of the church. Those who performed their functions well were worthy of *double honor.* Since the word *honor*…in this case means compensation, remuneration "that which is paid in honor of another's work" *double honor* probably refers to an honorarium or wage.[1]

Spiros Zodhiates' *Bible Word Study Dictionary* says this about double honor:

> Used in the sense of a price paid for something, it has been suggested here that it be translated, honorarium, but that raises the problem of double. Double what was paid the widows, or double what the other elders received? The New English Bible suggests, "reckoned worthy of a double stipend." One other states, "deserving twice the salary they get."[2]

It is clear that Paul is communicating a mentality of honoring leaders who sacrifice to minister to the people of God. He is stating that there should be some measure of financial reward for their labor. Again, this speaks of value and esteem. It also makes practical sense in so many ways that people who give their lives to the ministry and do it well should have more than enough.

God's ministers should be well cared for. We should realize that sowing and giving into their lives is part of God's kingdom mentality. We should also renew our minds and recognize that providing strong salaries for the ministry gifts is biblical. Recently I saw people debating on social media the concept of giving honorariums to speakers who travel. Of course I realize that some people tend to be over the top, and some even abuse these things. But it saddens me to think that anyone would want God's powerful ministers to struggle. We need prophets, and we want evangelists to till the ground and pray our families into the kingdom. So why would we give them inadequate offerings and send them on their way?

We *can* and *should* do better!

Belief is empowered by investment. This is true on every front, including the financial front. Sowing and giving are signs of honor. We sow into visions we believe in. Even those whose thinking is ungodly follow this principle. If you analyze their banking habits and how they spend their money, you discover what they care about. People invest in the things, places, and people they love. They spend their money on that which they value.

Though the passage from 1 Timothy 5 deals with financial honor, there are additional ways to express honor. We can honor people and leaders with intercession. There is no greater gift than prayer. Many leaders are taken out by demonic onslaughts. They need strong intercession. The prayers of God's people can thwart the attacks of the enemy.

Serving is a form of honor. Some give their lives for the causes in which they believe. When we love a ministry and serve the leader's vision, we are making an investment. No ministry or leader can get the job done alone. In the early church the willingness of God's people contributed to the multiplication that occurred. Many churches and powerful ministries stall out because the people do not honor the vision or anointing by serving.

Paul made a deeply spiritual point about double honor. Those who teach, preach, prophesy, and devote their lives to the people of God should be honored in giving and other forms of support. Too many people stay on the receiving end where ministry is concerned. We need to be intentional in sowing into the leaders and ministries that make a difference.

Sowing into people brings you God's glory. So honor the price they have paid with a demonstration of honor—your seed.

Chapter 5

TWO TIMES TWO

THE CONCEPT OF the double-double is one of multiplication and fruitfulness. It is about embracing God's power to prosper in every area of your life. What would happen to you with double-double productivity, creativity, ideas, prophetic insight, financial harvest, or ministerial reach? And how do you enter the realm of multiplication?

It's simple: you have to shake off the heaviness and the lies of the enemy. You must renew your mind, break old thought patterns, and plunge deep into the power of God.

From the very beginning God desired His kids to prosper and be fruitful!

> Then God said, "Let Us make man in Our image, according to Our likeness; and let them rule over the fish of the sea and over the birds of the sky and over the cattle and over

> all the earth, and over every creeping thing
> that creeps on the earth." God created man in
> His own image, in the image of God He cre-
> ated him; male and female He created them.
> God blessed them; and God said to them, "Be
> fruitful and multiply, and fill the earth, and
> subdue it; and rule over the fish of the sea and
> over the birds of the sky and over every living
> thing that moves on the earth."
>
> —GENESIS 1:26–28

God commissioned us to be fruitful. There was no plan for barrenness! The ordination of heaven was to bear supernatural fruit and walk in dominion. This was God's intent for His creation. Man was also instructed to multiply. The enemy opposes God's plan by limiting our fruit and stealing the power of rapid increase. He does his best to frustrate us and stall us out.

THE CHALLENGE TO OBEY

In Elisha's day a debt-saddled widow who'd already suffered greatly faced a fierce attack and stood to lose everything.

> Now a certain woman of the wives of the
> sons of the prophets cried out to Elisha, "Your
> servant my husband is dead, and you know
> that your servant feared the LORD; and the

creditor has come to take my two children to be his slaves." Elisha said to her, "What shall I do for you? Tell me, what do you have in the house?" And she said, "Your maidservant has nothing in the house except a jar of oil." Then he said, "Go, borrow vessels at large for yourself from all your neighbors, even empty vessels; do not get a few. And you shall go in and shut the door behind you and your sons, and pour out into all these vessels, and you shall set aside what is full." So she went from him and shut the door behind her and her sons; they were bringing the vessels to her and she poured. When the vessels were full, she said to her son, "Bring me another vessel." And he said to her, "There is not one vessel more." And the oil stopped. Then she came and told the man of God. And he said, "Go, sell the oil and pay your debt, and you and your sons can live on the rest."

—2 KINGS 4:1–7

This widow was in a dire situation. Her husband had died and left behind insurmountable debt. It was a dilemma she could not imagine herself overcoming. What would she do? How would she get over this? On top of the financial ruin she faced the devastating possibility that her sons would be taken captive and enslaved to pay the debt.

This story reveals the devil's ruthless nature. Anytime I see someone facing a spiritual attack, it strikes on multiple fronts. As it did for the widow, the siege comes through natural circumstances, hitting the heart and emotions. It comes rapidly and with intense fire. I can only imagine the level of despair this woman must have felt. On top of it all, her late husband had been a prophet. This set of circumstances should not have been her reality!

Many times we face things that are simply not fair. Yet there is still a promise. Sometimes we just have to look much harder to see the promise and remember it.

God sent the widow a prophet with a miracle mantle. Prophets and prophetic words often unlock miracles. Elisha knew that. He asked the woman what she had in her house. I am sure the question puzzled her, as it seemed to have nothing to do with her crisis. Prophets are peculiar, and their questions are often challenging. She had some oil and a few vessels. It seemed like nothing considering the problem, but when multiplication hit, it became more than enough.

Perhaps you find yourself facing a dire situation now. Maybe you look around and feel as if you do not have what it takes. Well, let me encourage you. When the double-double shows up, little becomes much!

The woman had a choice—the same choice you and I face. Would she simply surrender to the pressure of the attack, or would she partner with heaven's instruction? Miracles require acts of obedience that sometimes challenge us to the very core. Fortunately the widow chose to listen to the prophet and heed his instruction.

She took the plunge and obeyed the word he brought—and multiplication showed up on every front! As she poured, the oil was doubled and then doubled again. She was walking in the double-double! The oil just kept flowing and flowing because the power of the word was flowing. This was not just natural oil; it was pure prophetic anointing flowing and impacting everything in the woman's life. Her entire debt was canceled, and her sons remained free!

The double-double disrupts and shatters the plans of the enemy.

Chapter 6

BLOODLINE BLESSINGS

THE DOUBLE GOD provided for the widow in 2 Kings 4 was not only for her but for her entire family. The double is not just about you. It is about blessing generations to come. Heaven wants to bless you so strongly that your grandchildren feel the impact.

Likewise the warfare is not just about you. It is about your entire bloodline. God wants you to come into so much favor and freedom that your whole family gets delivered. This is the power of the double-double: blessings on top of blessings.

God has promised blessing from the beginning. He clearly promised it to the father of the faith.

> For when God made the promise to Abraham, since He could swear by no one greater, He swore by Himself, saying, "I will surely bless you and I will surely multiply you."
>
> —HEBREWS 6:13–14

God did not want to bless Abraham alone; He wanted to multiply the blessing Abraham received! He wanted to bless him so hugely that his descendants would come under the weight of the blessing. In fact, the power of God's covenant with Abraham is still active today.

The promises of God are generational! As you come under the promise of the double-double, there is power to bless and impact generations yet to come.

> Praise the LORD! How blessed is the man who fears the LORD, who greatly delights in His commandments. His descendants will be mighty on earth; the generation of the upright will be blessed. Wealth and riches are in his house, and his righteousness endures forever.
>
> —PSALM 112:1–3

For those planted in God's kingdom, the promise of the Lord is that their descendants will be mighty upon the earth. As men and women of God decide to seek and honor Him, their families are positioned for kingdom blessings. Then their obedience unlocks multiplied blessings, favor, and increase—and God's kingdom plans for the generations are multiplied. God is faithful to keep covenant with your children and grandchildren.

BLOODLINE BREAKERS

We often use the term *bloodline breaker* to describe a man or woman who has been rescued from darkness and brought into the plans of God. Once the bloodline breaker has been ransomed, he or she boldly and unashamedly stands upon the Word of God for the salvation and deliverance of the next generations, because God deals with covenants and generations.

> God said, "This is the sign of the covenant which I am making between Me and you and every living creature that is with you, for all successive generations."
>
> —GENESIS 9:12

The Lord is a generational God who keeps His promises. So many times we feel left out or alone because family members are not yielding to God's promise. Yet we are marked to be forerunners in the promises of God. We need to square our shoulders and walk with confidence, knowing that we serve a God who breaks curses and redeems the broken, as the Scriptures reveal:

> Christ redeemed us from the curse of the Law, having become a curse for us—for it is written, "Cursed is everyone who hangs on a tree"— in order that in Christ Jesus the blessing of Abraham might come to the Gentiles, so that

we would receive the promise of the Spirit through faith.

—GALATIANS 3:13–14

"No weapon that is formed against you will prosper; and every tongue that accuses you in judgment you will condemn. This is the heritage of the servants of the LORD, and their vindication is from Me," declares the LORD.

—ISAIAH 54:17

If anyone is in Christ, he is a new creature; the old things passed away; behold, new things have come.

—2 CORINTHIANS 5:17

The dictionary defines *bloodline* as "a sequence of direct ancestors especially in a pedigree"[1] and lists the following synonyms: "ancestry, birth, blood, breeding, descent, extraction, family tree, genealogy, line, lineage, origin, parentage, pedigree."[2]

Do you see the picture that is emerging? God is not just speaking of deliverance for you and your immediate family. He is speaking of a double-double that hits your entire family tree! He has saved you and raised you up as a bloodline breaker. You are called to pray, decree, and prophesy over your family.

God chose you to be His intercessor for your

bloodline. He chose you to stand against every evil desire and decree over it. He ransomed you and brought you forth into His glory, power, and abundance. He is rich in mercy toward your family.

> But God, being rich in mercy, because of His great love with which He loved us, even when we were dead in our transgressions, made us alive together with Christ (by grace you have been saved), and raised us up with Him, and seated us with Him in the heavenly places in Christ Jesus, so that in the ages to come He might show the surpassing riches of His grace in kindness toward us in Christ Jesus. For by grace you have been saved through faith; and that not of yourselves, it is the gift of God; not as a result of works, so that no one may boast. For we are His workmanship, created in Christ Jesus for good works, which God prepared beforehand so that we would walk in them.
>
> —EPHESIANS 2:4–10

Expect the double-double for your family. Expect the double-double over your entire bloodline. Boldly stand and declare the mercy, favor, and power of God over them. This is part of God's rich plan of multiplication for your generations.

Chapter 7

SEE INTO the LIMITLESS

To ENTER THE double-double for your life, you have to break free from limitations. Limited thinking will always box you in and cause you to reduce the size of your dreams. This is the work of the enemy. He wants to shut you off from the unlimited resources of heaven. The devil wants to subtract from your life to block creative imaginations that partner with the possibilities of heaven. This is the power of hell in action.

The story of Moses' twelve spies illustrates my point.

> Then the LORD spoke to Moses saying, "Send out for yourself men so that they may spy out the land of Canaan, which I am going to give to the sons of Israel; you shall send a man from each of their fathers' tribes, every one a leader among them." So Moses sent them from the wilderness of Paran at the command

of the LORD, all of them men who were heads
of the sons of Israel.

—NUMBERS 13:1–3

Bear in mind that before Moses sent men to spy out
Canaan, God's people had received His assurance that
the Promised Land would be theirs. Once they saw the
land and its fruit, they knew it was as good as God had
said it would be.

> When they returned from spying out the
> land, at the end of forty days, they proceeded
> to come to Moses and Aaron and to all the
> congregation of the sons of Israel in the wil-
> derness of Paran, at Kadesh; and they brought
> back word to them and to all the congrega-
> tion and showed them the fruit of the land.
>
> Thus they told him, and said, "We went in
> to the land where you sent us; and it certainly
> does flow with milk and honey, and this is
> its fruit. Nevertheless, the people who live in
> the land are strong, and the cities are forti-
> fied and very large; and moreover, we saw the
> descendants of Anak there. Amalek is living
> in the land of the Negev and the Hittites and
> the Jebusites and the Amorites are living in
> the hill country, and the Canaanites are living
> by the sea and by the side of the Jordan."
>
> Then Caleb quieted the people before

Moses and said, "We should by all means go up and take possession of it, for we will surely overcome it." But the men who had gone up with him said, "We are not able to go up against the people, for they are too strong for us." So they gave out to the sons of Israel a bad report of the land which they had spied out, saying, "The land through which we have gone, in spying it out, is a land that devours its inhabitants; and all the people whom we saw in it are men of great size. There also we saw the Nephilim (the sons of Anak are part of the Nephilim); and we became like grasshoppers in our own sight, and so we were in their sight."

—NUMBERS 13:25–33

Despite everything they knew to be true, the children of Israel reduced God to the size of their vision! They could not see past the obstacles, and they saw themselves as grasshoppers! They bowed to the spirit of limitation and aborted the plans of heaven for their lives. God had already spoken to them, but they allowed fear to overtake them.

They missed the double-double!

In the end only two of the twelve, Caleb and Joshua, rose up and declared the report of the Lord. (See Numbers 14:6–9.) Everyone else was influenced by the evil report. That's what the spirit of limitation does—it brings evil reports and fearful visions in an attempt to hold you back from God's appointed multiplication for your life, ministry, family, and finances.

This is why you must be cautious about what you see and hear. If you listen to negative reports and continually allow the wrong people to talk to you, they will contaminate your faith. Their negativity will influence you and get you to settle for much less than what God has promised. This is the target of the spirit of limitation. It comes to shrink your vision.

Be very cautious about what you set in front of your eyes. Don't watch and entertain negative things all the time. This will impact your mind and emotions. Your imagination is the birthing ground of increase and the double. If the enemy can contaminate your imagination, he can limit your reach and stop you from rising to the levels that heaven has already declared over your life.

Notice that people operating under a spirit of limitation are restricted even though God has placed them in the land of plenty. This was the Israelites' condition after the spies' evil report. It contaminated them with unbelief, which is like a cancer that rapidly spreads and attempts to topple the plans of God.

It takes faith to lay hold upon the promises of God. It takes faith to dream the dreams of God. It takes faith to stretch out and reach higher. It takes faith to soar! Faith comes by clearly hearing God's voice and trusting in His leading.

> So faith comes from hearing, and hearing by the word of Christ.
>
> —ROMANS 10:17

THINK LIKE GOD

The early church didn't just move in addition; it moved in multiplication! By the power of the Holy Spirit the people stepped into a supernatural advance. They were mobilized, activated, and accelerated. A tremendous revival birthed new converts, released the miraculous, and saw uncommon healings and phenomenal deliverances. Having burst forth from the upper room, they experienced nothing less than explosive growth!

This growth was about people—people who heard the message of Christ and were being transformed in ways that most had not expected. As Peter preached his fiery sermon on the day of Pentecost, people responded in droves.

> Now when they heard this, they were pierced to the heart, and said to Peter and the rest of the apostles, "Brethren, what shall we do?" Peter said to them, "Repent, and each of you be baptized in the name of Jesus Christ for the forgiveness of your sins; and you will

receive the gift of the Holy Spirit. For the promise is for you and your children and for all who are far off, as many as the Lord our God will call to Himself." And with many other words he solemnly testified and kept on exhorting them, saying, "Be saved from this perverse generation!"

So then, those who had received his word were baptized; and that day there were added about three thousand souls. They were continually devoting themselves to the apostles' teaching and to fellowship, to the breaking of bread and to prayer. Everyone kept feeling a sense of awe; and many wonders and signs were taking place through the apostles.

ACTS 2:37–43

God chose the very disciple who denied Jesus to be a leader on the front lines of this new move! When Peter denied the Lord, he was under a blanket of fear and intimidation. But when he emerged from the upper room, there was something different about him. Peter had a new boldness! The Spirit of God had baptized him in radical fire and power. He preached with no fear.

At least three thousand new converts came into the kingdom after hearing a single message! This was the beginning of a revolution that would shake the known world. The church was birthed in fire and glory. It would emerge under the power of exponential multiplication and sweep the territories. As the church moved in miracles and power, cities were changed, regions were transformed, and lives were forever marked by the passion and love of Jesus Christ.

Multiplication is God's plan for you and me! He wants us to expect and believe for supernatural increase and expansion. We cannot stay small in the midst of His presence. He is releasing us into the double-double! It is time to expect, believe, and decree the double-double in every area of our lives, no matter how "small" we feel.

> A little one shall become a thousand, and a small one a strong nation: I the LORD will hasten it in his time.
>
> —ISAIAH 60:22, KJV

This is how God thinks. He can take the little ones— the despised, rejected, or frustrated ones—and raise them up.

Isaiah was writing to the people of God, and it applies to us today. In that verse the word *nation* includes the idea of a tribe or a clan. In other words, God is going to heal us from rejection and establish us with the right people (or tribe) in His kingdom. He will raise us up by the power of His Spirit. The Lord desires to make of His people a strong nation!

Let's remember that we are dealing with the redemptive nature of God's glory. He says we will arise in the midst of His glory—His very presence—where promotion and favor come forth. In the midst of His presence, the impossible is possible and purposes are ignited.

Meditate on Isaiah 60:22, and claim it over your life. It reveals the double-double principle. God can make the small one mighty.

Chapter 8

PRAYERS and INCREASE DECREES

M Y PRAYER IS that the preceding pages have spoken to your heart and deeply encouraged and empowered you. Now it's time for you to speak aloud—in prayer to God and in decreeing His truth over your life.

Included between the following prayer and the closing decree for the double-double, you will find nine topical increase decrees accompanied by Scripture verses. Reading about the double-double has already stirred your heart. Now it's time to add fuel to the fire by speaking.

> *Father, I thank You that as I've read these words, my faith has been coming alive for the double-double! I thank You that according to Ephesians 3, You can do exceedingly abundantly above all that I can*

> *ask or even think. I take all limitations off*
> *my thinking, my believing, and my mind-*
> *set. I confess double in my life! I receive this*
> *word, and I believe it. I will no longer live*
> *with a mind-set of lack or bondage. I take*
> *off the limits and release freedom in my life.*
> *In Jesus' name, amen.*

So be it! Now let this verse soak your spirit and remind you that the double-double is not hard for God.

> Now unto him that is able to do exceeding
> abundantly above all that we ask or think,
> according to the power that worketh in us,
> unto him be glory in the church by Christ
> Jesus throughout all ages, world without end.
> Amen.
>
> —EPHESIANS 3:20–21, KJV

INCREASE DECREES

The increase you want is not limited to finances. Kingdom increase touches every area of your life. As your heart opens to receiving various aspects of God's blessing, the possibilities expand exponentially.

Wisdom

> Happy is the man that findeth wisdom, and
> the man that getteth understanding. For the

merchandise of it is better than the merchandise of silver, and the gain thereof than fine gold. She is more precious than rubies: and all the things thou canst desire are not to be compared unto her.

—PROVERBS 3:13–15, KJV

I decree wisdom in my life. I say that I am increasing in wisdom and understanding. I confess that I walk in the supernatural wisdom of God. I say that I am growing in wisdom and understanding daily. Wisdom is increasing in my life. I am moving into greater realms and levels of wisdom. I see solutions where others see problems. I have ideas when others are empty. I see strategies when others see dead ends. My mind is renewed and filled with God thoughts. I say that wisdom is my portion, and I decree more wisdom. I receive and walk in the spirit of wisdom and revelation. In Jesus' name, amen.

Favor

My son, do not forget my teaching, but let your heart keep my commandments; for length of days and years of life and peace they will add to you. Do not let kindness and truth leave you; bind them around your neck, write them on the tablet of your heart. So you will find favor and good repute in the sight of God and man.

—PROVERBS 3:1–4

I decree an increase of favor in my life. I say that I am at the right place at the right time. I say that I am increasing in favor with God and man. The right people like me. The right doors open for me. The right timing is unfolded for me. I am not ahead or behind. I walk in perfect timing. I walk in divine favor. In Jesus' name, amen.

Understanding

Consider what I say, for the Lord will give you understanding in everything.

—2 TIMOTHY 2:7

I decree increase in revelation and understanding. I say that I have the mind of Christ, and God's wisdom and understanding are working in me, through me, and for me. I am not led by my natural mind or emotions but by the Spirit of God. I have divine understanding and am increasing daily in revelation. In Jesus' name, amen.

Insight

> My son, if you will receive my words and treasure my commandments within you, make your ear attentive to wisdom, incline your heart to understanding; for if you cry for discernment, lift your voice for understanding; if you seek her as silver and search for her as for hidden treasures; then you will discern the fear of the LORD and discover the knowledge of God. For the LORD gives wisdom; from His mouth come knowledge and understanding.
>
> —PROVERBS 2:1–6

> *I decree that I am increasing in insight! I am increasing in the heavenly perspective. The spirit of wisdom is working in my life. I think God thoughts. I have kingdom strategies. I see things from heaven's perspective. In Jesus' name, amen.*

Health, Healing, and Deliverance

> He sent His word and healed them, and delivered them from their destructions.
>
> —PSALM 107:20

> *I decree an increase of healing and deliverance in my life. I decree that my body is*

healthy and I walk in divine health. I command sickness and disease to go from me now. I say that every fiber, tissue, organ, and gland in my body is normal. I confess that my cells are whole and healed. I confess that my bones are strong and normal. I release the healing power of God from the top of my head to the tips of my toes. I decree freedom and deliverance in my life. No demon can harass or torment me. I am not subject to demonic intimidation or attack. I walk in power and authority, and I confess freedom. In the mighty name of Jesus, amen.

Peace

Peace I leave with you; My peace I give to you; not as the world gives do I give to you. Do not let your heart be troubled, nor let it be fearful.
—JOHN 14:27

I decree an increase in the level of peace in my life. I walk in God's supernatural and glorious peace. I am not moved by the attacks or lies of the enemy. I am not intimidated or fearful. I am full of God's peace and joy. In Jesus' name, amen.

Relationships

> With all humility and gentleness, with patience, showing tolerance for one another in love, being diligent to preserve the unity of the Spirit in the bond of peace.
>
> —EPHESIANS 4:2–3

> *I decree increase in right relationships in my life. I confess the right people at the right time. I confess people who add to my life and are partners in my destiny. I break and bind all distractions in the area of relationships. In Jesus' name, amen.*

Ministry

> Jesus came up and spoke to them, saying, "All authority has been given to Me in heaven and on earth. Go therefore and make disciples of all the nations, baptizing them in the name of the Father and the Son and the Holy Spirit, teaching them to observe all that I commanded you; and lo, I am with you always, even to the end of the age."
>
> —MATTHEW 28:18–20

For a wide door for effective service has opened to me, and there are many adversaries.
—1 CORINTHIANS 16:9

I decree that I am sent as You lead me, and I declare increase in the ministry You have given me. I say that I am increasing in Your power, Lord. I am increasing in Your glory. I say that the right doors are opening and the wrong ones are closing. In Jesus' name, amen.

Finances

Those who seek the LORD shall not lack any good thing.

—PSALM 34:10, NKJV

Let them shout for joy and be glad, who favor my righteous cause; and let them say continually, "Let the LORD be magnified, who has pleasure in the prosperity of His servant."

—PSALM 35:27, NKJV

I decree the double-double over my finances. I say that I have more than enough. I walk in kingdom abundance in the name of Jesus. I decree increase in favor, increase in blessing, increase in ideas, increase in promotion, and increase in the flow of finances. I expect increase. I receive increase. I praise You, Lord, for financial increase. I say that I have more than enough. You take pleasure in my prosperity. You are causing doors of favor to open. You are causing raises and promotions to manifest. You are causing financial opportunities to open up. I prophesy abundance over my life. In Jesus' name, amen.

DECREE THE DOUBLE-DOUBLE

Double-double is mine.

Promotion is mine.

Wisdom is mine.

Favor is mine.

Insight and counsel belong to me.

I refuse to be limited or held back.

It is my time and season for great exploits.

I break lack.

I break fear.

I break worry.

I break distress.

I bind and break all demonic powers trying to cloud my mind.

I break confusion.

I break control.

I break limitation.

I release heaven's agenda.

I release heaven's glory.

I release heaven's healing.

I release the growing and expanding kingdom on earth.

I can do the impossible.

I can see the invisible.

I move in the supernatural.

I am a mountain mover.

I am a nation shaker and a city taker.

I am a child of the King, and royalty is my portion.

I am unstoppable and will not be defeated.

I rule in Jesus.

I reign in Jesus.

I prophesy by the power of Jesus.

I live by the faith of Jesus.

I move by the love of Jesus.

I am under the direct influence of heaven and all its splendor.

I do not think average, ordinary, or mundane thoughts.

My thinking is not limited.

I think big, bold, faith-filled thoughts.

My heart is filled with mega dreams.

I refuse to move backward.

I am moving forward.

I am walking in multiplication.

I am walking in wisdom.

I am walking in power.

I am walking in authority.

I am walking in the double-double!

As you have read these words, prayed these prayers, and spoken these decrees, I believe God has inspired you to believe for more! I sincerely believe that the loving heart of the Father is to empower you to do everything He has put you on earth to do.

It is impossible to achieve the destiny that heaven has for you without daring to believe.

Sometimes you simply must step beyond the ordinary, push back against the pressure, and leap forward! It won't feel normal or ordinary; the double-double never does. God is inviting you to come up higher in your thinking and dreaming. He is inviting you to change your perspective and see from a totally new vantage point.

Heaven does not intend for you to live under false limitations. Heaven expects you to boldly pray for *the more*. A whole group of pioneers and forerunners is cheering you on. Go for it!

This is the power of the double-double!

It is the power of increase in action.

Embrace the double-double!

NOTES

CHAPTER 1
GOD WILL MORE THAN RESTORE

1.   *Merriam-Webster*, s.v. "restore," accessed December 24, 2018, https://www.merriam-webster.com/dictionary/restore.

CHAPTER 3
THE DOUBLE PORTION

1.   *Merriam-Webster*, s.v. "shame," accessed December 24, 2018, https://www.merriam-webster.com/dictionary/shame.

CHAPTER 4
DOUBLE HONOR

1.   Forerunner Commentary, s.v. "1 Timothy 5:17," accessed December 24, 2018, https://www.bibletools.org/index.cfm/fuseaction/Bible.show/sVerseID/29781/eVerseID/2978.

2.   Forerunner Commentary, s.v. "1 Timothy 5:17."

CHAPTER 6
BLOODLINE BLESSINGS

1.   *Merriam-Webster*, s.v. "bloodline," accessed December 24, 2018, https://www.merriam-webster.com/dictionary/bloodline.

2.   *Merriam-Webster*, s.v. "bloodline."